# PR 2.0

## How Digital Media Can Help You
## Build a Sustainable Brand

## John Friedman
Huffington Post Sustainability blogger
and international business executive
**@JohnFriedman**

T0321002

First published in 2015 by Dō Sustainability

87 Lonsdale Road, Oxford OX2 7ET, UK

Copyright © 2015 John Friedman

The moral right of the author has been asserted.

ISBN 978-1-910174-42-5 (eBook-ePub)

ISBN 978-1-910174-43-2 (eBook-PDF)

ISBN 978-1-910174-41-8 (Paperback)

A catalogue record for this title is available from the British Library.

Dō Sustainability strives for net positive social and environmental impact. See our sustainability policy at **www.dosustainability.com**.

Page design and typesetting by Alison Rayner

Cover by Becky Chilcott

For further information on Dō Sustainability, visit our website: **www.dosustainability.com**

# DōShorts

**Dō Sustainability** is the publisher of **DōShorts**: short, high-value business guides that distill sustainability best practice and business insights for busy, results-driven professionals. Each DōShort can be read in 90 minutes.

## New and forthcoming DōShorts – stay up to date

We publish new DōShorts each month. The best way to keep up to date? Sign up to our short, monthly newsletter. Go to **www.dosustainability. com/newsletter** to sign up to the Dō Newsletter. Some of our latest and forthcoming titles include:

- *Networks for Sustainability: Harnessing People Power to Deliver Your Goals*   Sarah Holloway
- *Making Sustainability Matter: How To Make Materiality Drive Profit, Strategy and Communications*   Dwayne Baraka
- *Creating a Sustainable Brand: A Guide to Growing the Sustainability Top Line*   Henk Campher
- *Cultivating System Change: A Practitioner's Companion*   Anna Birney
- *How Much Energy Does Your Building Use?*   Liz Reason
- *Lobbying for Good: How Business Advocacy Can Accelerate the Delivery of a Sustainable Economy*   Paul Monaghan & Philip Monaghan
- *Creating Employee Champions: How to Drive Business Success Through Sustainability Engagement Training*   Joanna M. Sullivan
- *Smart Engagement: Why, What, Who and How*   John Aston & Alan Knight

- *How to Produce a Sustainability Report*   Kye Gbangbola & Nicole Lawler

- *Strategic Sustainable Procurement: An Overview of Law and Best Practice for the Public and Private Sectors*   Colleen Theron & Malcolm Dowden

- *The Reputation Risk Handbook: Surviving and Thriving in the Age of Hyper-Transparency*   Andrea Bonime-Blanc

- *Business Strategy for Water Challenges: From Risk to Opportunity*   Stuart Orr and Guy Pegram

- *Accelerating Sustainability Using the 80/20 Rule*   Gareth Kane

- *The Guide to the Circular Economy: Capturing Value and Managing Material Risk*   Dustin Benton, Jonny Hazell and Julie Hill

## Subscriptions

In addition to individual sales of our ebooks, we now offer subscriptions. Access 60+ ebooks for the price of 6 with a personal subscription to our full e-library. Institutional subscriptions are also available for your staff or students. Visit **www.dosustainability.com/books/subscriptions** or email **veruschka@dosustainability.com**

## Write for us, or suggest a DōShort

Please visit **www.dosustainability.com** for our full publishing programme. If you don't find what you need, write for us! Or suggest a DōShort on our website. We look forward to hearing from you.

# Abstract

**AT THE DAWN** of the 21st century, several trends have come together to transform how organizations effectively communicate with stakeholders.

1. First, the instant information age has irrevocably changed how people create, share, receive, judge and interact with information.

2. Second, the focus on transparency and authenticity driven by the emphasis on corporate responsibility has transformed the role of business communicators from developing and disseminating messages to engaging stakeholders.

3. Third, while "public relations" is often a synonym for "media relations," its real value is maximizing how an organization manages its relationships with its various publics.

4. Fourth, digital media offer many of the same attributes that make face-to-face the most effective form of communications; including interactivity, immediacy and the ability to establish relationships despite physical distances.

5. Lastly, the fragmentation of media audiences, increasing skepticism of traditional corporate messages and a digital-savvy workforce and consumer base necessitate that companies take advantage of the tools are available and use them most effectively.

# ABSTRACT

The true value of digital media can only be fully realized by leveraging these trends. This book presents effective and proven strategies to do so. I call this transformation PR 2.0.

..........................................................................................

# About the Author

 **JOHN FRIEDMAN** is an award-winning communications professional and recognized sustainability expert with more than 25 years of experience as both an external and internal sustainability leader, helping companies, ranging from small companies to leading global enterprises, turn their values into successful business models by integrating their environmental, social, and economic aspirations into their cultures and business practices.

@JohnFriedman is recognized as a thought leader on digital media; #2 on Triple Pundit's List of the Top 30 Sustainability Bloggers on Twitter http://www.triplepundit.com/2013/03/top-30-sustainability-bloggers-twitter/, #3 on GreenBiz list of most influential 'twitterati' http://www.greenbiz.com/blog/2014/08/13/greenbiz-twitterati-2014, #14 on Guardian Business' 30 most influential sustainability voices in America http://www.theguardian.com/sustainable-business/twitter-list-30-sustainability-voices-america and has regularly been included among the top voices in CSR by Forbes' Brandfog since 2010. His insights on sustainability issues and strategy are regular features on Huffington Post, and he hosts 'Sound Living with John Friedman' on EcoPlanetRadio.com. His pieces have also appeared on 3BLMedia, CSRwire, SustainableBrands, Forbes.com, Vaultcareers, and JustMeans.

An Albany State (New York) communications graduate, Friedman earned a management certificate as part of the Lafarge/Duke Management Training program at the Fuqua School of Business in 2000.

...................................................................................

# Contents

CHAPTER 1

# Introduction

........................................................................................

**FIGURE 1. Where do digital media fit?**

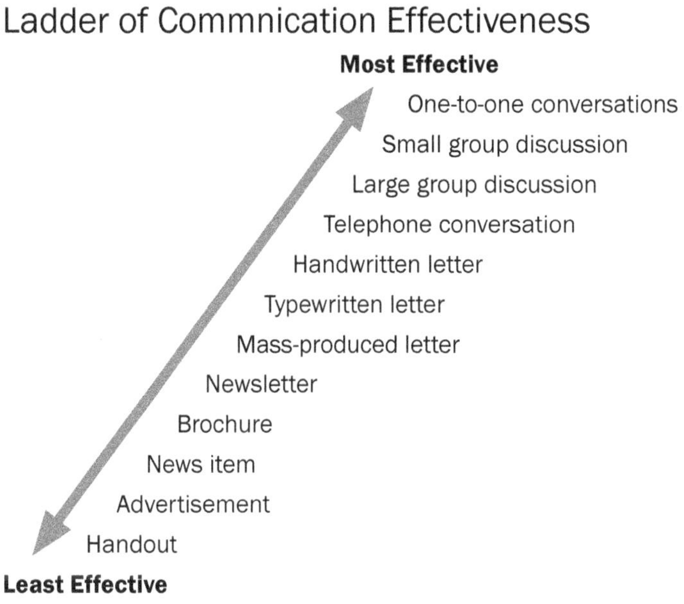

## Ladder of Commnication Effectiveness

**Most Effective**

One-to-one conversations

Small group discussion

Large group discussion

Telephone conversation

Handwritten letter

Typewritten letter

Mass-produced letter

Newsletter

Brochure

News item

Advertisement

Handout

**Least Effective**

Created in 1985 by the *Harvard Business Review*, before e-mail or digital media, the question now needs to be asked, and answered: 'Where do digital media like e-mail, Facebook, Twitter, Instagram, etc. belong on this graphic?'

........................................................................................

**AT THE 2014** Sustainable Brands conference in San Diego, protestors carrying signs and an increasing number of tweets from relatively few accounts should have served as a 'canary in the coalmine' for conference sponsor 3M. But when their VP of global sustainability took the main stage for a scheduled presentation, she stuck with her prepared script. As a result, conference attendees started weighing in via Twitter, even during her remarks. Comments ranged from questioning – 'Good social innovation talk from @3M, but curious made no mention of the forestry issues or protesters outside' – to the downright critical – '#3M #sustainability VP gave a speech at #SB14sd that didn't address controversial fiber in 3M's #supplychain' and 'I had a hard time ignoring this. How can they?' The story quickly expanded beyond the 2000 conference attendees. Both *Triple Pundit* and *Guardian Business* (two of the most widely respected and read publications for sustainability professionals) covered it on their blogs. *The Guardian* summed it up: 'At the very least, the right thing would have been to acknowledge this, but she didn't. When asked about it afterwards, she said she could not comment without clearance from the comms team.'[1] By failing to recognize the threat or the opportunity, 3M failed to engage in PR 2.0.

An activist organization announced on social media its plans to bring a celebrity to the corporate headquarters of a company it was attempting to protest. One of the directors in the public relations department, seeing the preparatory language on digital media, recommended that the company take a proactive course of action – instead of allowing the visual of the actor to be arrested, invite him into building to engage with the company. Ultimately the idea was rejected and so the activists were able to use video and photos from the event, and stories on their own blog for months afterward. Even though little traction was gained from it in the end, by failing to take advantage of digital media to redefine their actions, the company failed to engage in PR 2.0.

On the other hand, in 2009 when suicide bombs ripped through hotels including the JW Marriott in Jakarta, Indonesia, Marriott's communications swiftly issued a simple acknowledgement on Twitter, 'Gathering info now . . .', less than 90 minutes after the explosions. Soon other updates followed, and a little more than two and a half hours after the bombings, Bill Marriott, chairman and chief executive officer used his blog to address the situation, offering condolences, detailing the steps taken to evacuate the properties and treat the victims and listing the phone numbers for concerned families to inquire about guests.

In 2014, the Westboro Baptist Church announced its intention to picket Washington DC's Wilson High School in response to the school's Pride Day celebration, only a handful of demonstrators showed up. But in the same time period, nearly 1,000 students signed up for the counter-protest on Facebook and hundreds of students and community members, led by student organizers, were on hand to show their support for the school and its principal, out numbering the Westboro protestors 10 to one.

At the Business for Social Responsibility (BSR) Conference in late 2014, BSR added a strong digital component to the event, streaming video out from the event and using a Twitter hashtag (#BSR14) so people could follow along and exchange ideas; but they also added a second hashtag (#AskBSR14) so people – even those unable to attend and watching the video – were able to pose questions to the speakers and presenters. Having this separate channel made it easier for those on stage to 'see' the questions. BSR effectively used Twitter as an engagement platform rather than simply as a distribution channel.

Amyotrophic lateral sclerosis (ALS) is a serious progressive neuro-degenerative disease that affects nerve cells in the brain and the spinal cord. In 1939 baseball superstar Lou Gehrig announced he had the disease (famously stating 'today I consider myself the luckiest man on the face of the Earth' during his moving retirement speech). In the summer of 2014, thanks to the 'ALS Ice Bucket Challenge' digital media campaign, the disease was once again forefront in people's minds. The challenge involves people getting doused with buckets of ice water on video, posting that video to social media, and then nominating others to do the same, all in an effort to raise ALS awareness. Those who refuse to take the challenge are asked to make a donation to the ALS charity of their choice.

While the idea of people choosing to douse themselves with ice-cold water rather than giving to charity may initially strike one as odd, the idea caught on in a big way, with many opting to do both. ALS charities benefitted in a big way. By the end of summer the ALS Association had received more than US$100 million in donations compared to a fraction of that during the same time period the prior year. These donations not only came from existing donors; more than a million new people were inspired to give to the Association.[2] That illustrates the power of digital media, to expand one's reach beyond traditional groups and individuals.

These are examples of PR 2.0, using digital tools not to send messages to audiences, but to actively engage stakeholders. Whether responding to a crisis or proactively reaching out, these organizations have recognized and used the power of digital media as both a source of information as well as a cadre of tools to engage with (not speak to) stakeholders.

# CHAPTER 2

# The Information Revolution

**KEY POINTS:**

- Interaction is the key to building any relationship from associates and customers to online engagement

- Digital media share attributes – interactivity, immediacy, non-verbals – that make face-to-face communications effective.

- Digital media and the Web went to scale when it went from a 'push' mechanism to a forum for participation

As stated earlier, factors have combined to transform how organizations can – and increasingly should – effectively communicate with their stakeholders. The instant information age has irrevocably changed how people create, share, receive, judge and interact with information. At the same

> *The focus on transparency and authenticity driven by sustainability as a business model has transformed the role of business communicators from developing and disseminating carefully prepared messages to a model that requires true stakeholder engagement.*

time, focus on transparency and authenticity driven by sustainability as a business model has transformed the role of business communicators from developing and disseminating carefully prepared messages to a model that requires true stakeholder engagement.

It's not a new phenomenon, as the Marriott example cited earlier makes clear; some companies have embraced the new world of digital media effectively. But many others are using these powerful tools as an additional mechanism to speak to (rather than engage with) stakeholders. Some are still using their websites primarily as online versions of their marketing brochures, posting press releases (often in static formats like PDFs) and even using Twitter to spit out a flurry of 140 character 'sound bites' without a strategy for engagement.

For all the money being spent to develop and implement digital strategies to engage directly with publics, it is not working. In fact, it has been an abysmal failure. Public confidence in corporations to do the right thing remains shockingly low. *Forbes* reported in January 2014 that when asked whether they trusted business leaders to 'tell you the truth, regardless of how complex or unpopular it is,' only 20 percent of the public said yes. Just 21 percent said they trusted business leaders to 'make ethical and moral decisions,'[3]

This erosion of trust stems from many reasons – not the least of which are the examples of malfeasance associated with the housing market and economic collapses. Far more executives and businesses behave in ways that are exemplary – yet that does not balance the negative examples. Part of the problem that businesses have been ineffective in building trust, I believe, is because too many of them are using 21st-century tools in a manner more suited for the 20th. We know that the three most effective forms of human communication are 1) personal interaction, followed by 2) small and then 3) larger group interactions. Digital media offer mechanisms for each of these methods but too often companies and organizations resort to using them as little more that advertising, failing to take advantage of the true power of digital media.

As Julie Urlaub, managing partner and founder of Taiga Company – a sustainability consultant and no stranger to effective digital media – points out on her blog, 'Quite possibly, you may be acting from the traditional "push communications" styles of the past while failing to embrace the new, level playing field of social media in which everyone has a voice?'[4]

Henk Campher, Senior Vice President, Business & Social Purpose and Managing Director, Sustainability at Edelman PR agrees:

*The majority of them are still treating digital effort in the same way they treated the media in 1990 – pushing out messages. A small group are going beyond 1990 PR and trying to engage their key audiences. But these are truly limited and even then limited to a few getting it right on a channel or two instead of a consistent strategy.*

The PR 2.0 model was designed and has been successfully used by companies to build programs that engage the public effectively, taking advantage of the unique aspects, properties and strengths of digital media, while understanding, acknowledging and preparing for their weaknesses as well.

Because of the strong and increasing importance that the various publics – employees, customers, clients and communities – place on the environmental, social and economic impacts that an organization has, many of the duties traditionally associated with communications departments, such as building internal buy-in and enhancing reputational capital, require that the organization maximize the effective development, implementation, management and communication of sustainability efforts across its value chain. In other words, by focusing less on the more traditional discussions and descriptions of the products and services a company (or organization) produces, and more on the impacts (and therefore the value) that they have on people in their daily lives is a vital part of sustainability communications that leverages the power of digital engagement. Building a strong connection between your digital communications strategy and your sustainability efforts refocuses your thinking in order to more effectively engage with people about *what matters to them*.

As an example, a company leading the way in sustainability and social media communications is Ford Motor Company. Ford recently (2014) took over the top position on the Best Global Green Brands Report by Interbrand. This report examines the gap between corporate environmental practices and consumer's perception of those practices. Digital, as part of an overall marketing strategy, has played a part in closing the gap between what they are doing around sustainability and what consumers believe the company to be doing around these issues.

By teaming up with YouTube action sports star Devin Super Tramp, Ford illustrated how much their Ford Focus can do on a single tank of gas, using the informal video format to capture movement, imagery and invoke the imagination of views. It moves higher mileage (fuel efficiency) from a numerical concept to literally in 'driving' hands of consumers with active imaginations, and showing them how they can 'try sustainability on', creatively.

'The role of social media shares similar values to sustainability: authenticity, transparency, and engagement. Noticeably, all of which are key characteristics which build trust and authentic real relationships', explains Urlaub.

Another company that is leading the way on building trust using social media is Unilever. The personal care product and food conglomerate has dozens of brands and thousands of products – Ben and Jerry's, Dove, Q tips, Suave, Lipton, Klondike. Having so many brands makes its sustainability program both extremely important and difficult to communicate, because it spans issues from health and hygiene to greenhouse gas reductions. Yet, Unilever has managed to bundle them all under one umbrella, the Unilever Sustainable Living Plan. The plan includes a multifaceted plan for communicating progress through a wide variety of methods, from video to Facebook to Twitter chats. It also includes traditional advertising tactics and public awareness campaigns including Dove's Real Beauty campaign which shares the message, 'You are more beautiful than you think.' These videos show the difference between how women describe themselves and how others describe them, by having an artist sketch based on what each says. What is important to note here is the different social media platforms used by Unilever to illustrate what sustainability means to their organization. By engaging in different ways – a Twitter chat or a video – it builds trust with consumers, suppliers, investors and the broader community.

Indeed, while public relations has been a synonym for media relations, if one takes the meaning of the words 'public' and 'relations' to mean how an organization manages its relationships with its various stakeholder publics, the argument can be made that the connection between sustainability and corporate communications goes beyond the philosophical; it is a strategic necessity.

.......................................................................................................................

# CHAPTER 3
# Sustainability as a Business Strategy

**KEY POINTS:**

- The business benefits of sustainability are real and they include the cultural mindset of authenticity and transparency.

- Tangible assets add up to less than half of any company's value; majority is stakeholder goodwill which sustainability helps generate.

- Effective management of stakeholder relationships requires that it be measured.

Most companies envy the passionate loyalty that Apple customers have for their products, or the dedication that Southwest Airlines employees demonstrate for their company. Effectively managing their relationships with these stakeholders is the key to earning these benefits. Employee engagement and customer loyalty are intangible (non-physical) assets that contribute more to the value of a company than the physical 'things' it owns.

According to research by Robert A.G. Monks and Alexandra Reed Lajoux, fully 80 percent of the market value of Standards and Poors 500 companies comes from intangible assets.[5] In 2005 Apple's market value was US$58 billion. The total tangible assets on its balance sheet –

> *80% of the market value of companies is contained in relationships with its stakeholders*

19.8 percent of that. 80.2 percent of the company's value was contained in its relationships with its stakeholders.

Each relationship is an intangible asset of the business. As any accountant will tell you, assets can appreciate, depreciate or hold their value.

By effectively managing relationships with increasing the opportunities and lowering the risk for each relationship, a company can enhance the quality of its intangible assets and therefore increase the overall valuation of the business. And later when we talk about how to 'sell' your strategy to business leaders, we will focus on this important aspect because business leaders know this (See Chapter 8: Building an Internal Constituency Including Selling It Upstairs).

So then the question becomes how to effectively manage your relationships with customers, employees, owners/investors, suppliers, competitors, communities and government agencies and regulators?

For each group the principles of integrity, authenticity and engagement (engaging in open dialogue rather than treating them as audiences who receive information) apply. And digital media offer avenues for each of these stakeholder groups.

**Customers**: Want, demand and deserve a superior customer experience; and often that means engaging with them about their concerns and desires. It means having a customer-friendly website that provides access to information and a timely and tailored response to inquiries. It also means responding to comments, questions and concerns in a timely fashion. Just as in a personal conversation, people expect a response rather than waiting until the perfectly worded statement can be crafted, as was mentioned earlier in the Marriott example. It is better to respond quickly and forthrightly than to wait until you have all the details.

Between 60 and 70 percent of consumers say that they are searching for 'greener' products, according to the latest research from the Shelton Group[6] but two things stand in the way of accessing this huge market. First, the price premium remains a barrier. Consumers are buying 'greener' consumables – particularly items in the low-cost and low-risk category. People are willing to purchase things like 'green' cleaning products that cost approximately 30 cents more (but are understandably more reluctant to spend US$30,000 on a new solar electricity system). The opportunity for companies is once they try the product they continue to do so for those items that give them a favorable experience.

The second barrier, and a trend that Shelton describes as 'really compelling,' is that consumer attitudes have shifted from looking at 'green' products to 'green' companies. Five years ago the environmental reputation of the company was the eighth most important factor in green product decision-making. Today it is second. So an effective communications program that shows how the company is fully committed to being 'green' is necessary, indeed essential to reach this large number of consumers.

Getting the majority of consumers to purchase 'green' products has been – and remains – an unfulfilled promise of sustainability efforts. But this research confirms that it is not because people have overestimated the size of the market interested in these goods, but because *they have failed to communicate* effectively with consumers in a way that demonstrates to them that the company shares their values.

**Employees**: As I said earlier, your brand reputation is the most **valuable** asset of your company. Your employees are, or should be, the most **valued**. This is more than a semantic difference. When something is valuable it is often hidden away, kept safe and away from prying eyes. But when something is truly valued it is showcased and highlighted – such as when Southwest Airlines encourages its flight attendants to customize the preflight safety announcements. This does not mean that they do not take passenger safety seriously – quite the reverse. They recognize that flight attendants are in a unique position to gauge whether or not passengers are paying attention to the information that could save their life in the unlikely event something goes wrong. And by demonstrating to their employees that they are trusted to deliver this potentially life-saving information in a manner that fits their personality and the situation, flight attendants are empowered and treated as valued assets. Compare this to the impersonal videos that other airlines simply play, checking off the 'we did that' box and engaging neither passengers nor crew in the information.

The best way to demonstrate to employees how the work they are doing is appreciated by their colleagues and important to customers is by showing them how their role fits into the larger picture. Focus on why what they do matters, not just what they make. An example of this is pointing out the difference between what the company makes (its products or services) and the impact those products and services have on people's lives – right in their own community whenever possible. A consistent theme running through *Working Mother*'s annual list of Best Places to

Work is that top employers invest in employee growth, engagement and satisfaction. That's how you invest in this valued asset.

**Owners/investors**: A return on investment is critically important to owners and investors but very often the 'need to satisfy the market' is used to justify short-term decisions that yield faster returns even at the expense of long-term viability. The critical flaw in this – one that has exerted an oversized and negative influence on corporate decision-makers – is that by listening to short-term investors who have the least (if any) interest in the long-term viability of your organization, you are being encouraged engage in actions that may compromise your long-term success. It is time that we recognized that if someone does not care about your long-term success (or health or well-being), by definition, they are not a stakeholder.

People who own the stock for a longer term are more interested in your long-term success. Owners understand this and that is one of the reasons for stock options for executives – it encourages long-term thinking (especially if the options have a window when they can be exercised).

> *When someone does not care about your long-term success (or health or well-being), by definition, they are not a stakeholder.*

**Suppliers**: A company's suppliers are critical to their success. The quality of the products that go into what you manufacture has a direct impact on the quality of the products that go to market bearing your brand. Making the right choice can enhance a company's reputation and increase the value of its brand. Making the wrong choice can have a devastating impact – as Toyota discovered when it outsourced its throttle mechanisms that were ultimately implicated in cases of uncontrolled acceleration of some of their vehicles. Suddenly their core value of safety and quality was threatened not by their own products, but by the products of others that they were integrating into their vehicles. Likewise, the taint of products made in unsafe conditions by people who are not being paid a living wage, for example, cannot be 'cleaned' once they enter your control. That is why companies must be sure to seek partners who share their commitments for reducing their environmental footprint, preserving and protecting human rights and a host of other issues, if they want their consumers to favor them for these attributes. In short – if you ask others to buy based on corporate responsibility values, doing anything less yourself is hypocritical.

**Communities**: Anyone who has tried and failed to get a business permit knows the power of local communities. They need to buy you before you get a chance to sell them anything. Despite the promise of jobs, products and contributing to the tax base, local people have protested and ultimately prevented major corporations from coming into their community. Managing your relationship with the community on the other hand, so that they see you as a benefit to the community, can result in public hearings where people speak on your behalf and expedited permits.

**Government regulators and legislators**: Think about your last auto inspection – if there's black smoke pouring out of your tailpipe, chances are it is going to take longer (and cost more money) than if the computer chip download shows emissions within acceptable parameters. In the same way, environmental inspectors very quickly know if they have entered a cleaner operation. Likewise, safety inspectors from the US Occupational Health and Safety Administration (OSHA) can recognize a safe and clean operation and engage in a thorough inspection that takes less time and is less disruptive.

And finally, **your competitors**: An often overlooked stakeholder group for any company are its competitors, because often the actions of one player can influence the image of an entire industry (or business in general). The oil spill associated with BP in the Gulf of Mexico resulted in a moratorium on all drilling, by all companies and damaged the image of safety and environmental responsibility of the entire industry. While most people understand and accept that every industry has its own issues relating to the environment, social and even economic responsibility, the absence of comparable standards across industry sectors means that business scandals (Enron, Worldcom and Arthur Anderson) sent shock waves through our entire society to the point where business and industry in general are distrusted.

The common theme through all these stakeholder groups is that they each need to be engaged not by what matters most to you, but through what matters most to *them.*

| Stakeholder | What they want to know | Digital engagement approach |
| --- | --- | --- |
| Customers | • Your organization shares their values, in actions as well as words<br>• To be treated as important, responding to their needs/concerns | • Reflect your values in how you engage online, fan pages, contests, etc.<br>• Respond quickly to issues raised, proactively whenever possible (and it's faster and cheaper than advertising) |
| Employees | • They matter and are respected<br>• How what they do (and the manner they do it) matters in the 'big picture' | • Empower them and turn them loose to do their best<br>• Show them how their efforts fit into the big picture by showcasing them on websites, employee profiles, etc. |
| Investors | • Their best interests are being served<br>• They can expect a strong return on their investment | • Let honesty and transparency be your guides |
| Suppliers | • The values you express to your consumers are the same as the ones you reward with your purchasing decisions | • Feature your suppliers in online publications, engage in online events just as you would in joint presentations at conferences |

| Stakeholder | What they want to know | Digital engagement approach |
|---|---|---|
| Communities | • You are a valuable and engaged part of the community and how | • Participate in online communities that reflect the local geographic community, be present digitally as well as physically |
| Regulators/ legislators | • Your values go beyond words but to actions | • Transparency and authenticity demonstrate that you 'have nothing to hide' but also that you have a lot to 'showcase'<br><br>• Share your 'best' safety, environmental, labor achievements |
| Competitors | • You are a responsible competitor that advances the industry and conducts business in a way that will not bring regulatory, legislative, pr or other shame to your industry | • Transparency and authenticity demonstrate that you 'have nothing to hide' but also that you have a lot to 'showcase' |

# CHAPTER 4

# The Powerful Combination of Living Your Values and Telling Your Authentic Story

**KEY POINTS:**

- Stakeholders don't expect perfection; but they are demanding honesty and fidelity in communications.

- You can recover from a mistake far more quickly than from a lie.

- Transparency is scary until you realize that people already know.

The shift from information dissemination to collaboration has been in process for some time. When organizations first began their tentative steps in using the internet, they largely used it as another distribution channel. While there were some nods to the unique attributes of the new technology, like the use of hyperlinks to allow users to control navigation, these early efforts largely remained one-way communications *to* a passive audience.

As Dr Wayne Visser, Director of the think-tank Kaleidoscope Futures and founder of CSR International points out:

> *In the first version of the Internet we were effectively putting our brochures on line, it was one-way communication. Now it's all*

*about user-generated content, interactivity, constant innovation,
beta-testing, and so on.*[7]

By the time that the Web went to scale; from 46 million users in 1996 to more than a billion in 2006, it had become far more interactive. Now the true power of user-generated content, interactivity and constant innovation have changed the way people experience the Internet. It is no longer a source of content-driven information, it is now an experiential space, were people interact – and expect to interact – with information, individuals and companies.

Just as baby-boomers ushered in 'business casual' attire to the workplace (much to the discomfort of traditionalists who adhered to the 'dress for success' model of emulating their supervisors), today's business leaders may find themselves challenged by workers and customers who, growing up with information 'in their hands' 24 hours a day, seven days a week, expect them to engage in real time. In the workplace and increasingly on digital media, customers expect companies not only to respond to them, but they expect it to be fast.

Another complication is the prevalence and importance of non-traditional digital media as sources of information and the increasing influence of bloggers and other citizen-journalists who increasingly have a great deal of credibility and reach.

These changes have fundamentally changed stakeholder expectations and, as a result, traditional communications functions are being redefined. Organizations that wish to communicate with credibility are moving from the familiar model of 'message delivery' toward 'transparency,' inviting (and sometimes hosting) conversations. They are being driven to be more

> *People are prepared to forgive a mistake, if you're forthright about it. What they won't forgive is if you lie or attempt to cover it up.*
>
> *And in many cases it is essentially a no-risk proposition – because you're 'fessing up to something that people already know.*

open about their aspirations and their efforts to achieve them; sometimes even acknowledging their shortcomings. Stakeholders are not asking for perfection; rather they're expecting honesty and fidelity in communications. People are prepared to forgive you for a mistake, if you're forthright about it. What they won't forgive is if you lie or attempt to cover it up. And those who do so find it is much easier to weather the storm.

JetBlue's Jenny Dervin, director of corporate communications, explained this for the Crisis Management Blog when describing the effect of an ice storm in 2007: 'Other airlines stopped flying, but JetBlue did not. We were only seven years old. Our operational decisions hadn't yet caught up with our size, and we were caught with our pants down.'

The company actually went as far to send email notes of apology to every one of its customers, and it announced a customer bill of rights detailing compensation in the event of future problems. 'We got out in front and asked people to forgive us', she explained. 'It's important to realize that customers want to hear an explanation only after you apologize.'[8]

What Dervin and JetBlue realized – and put into practice – was that communications professionals are no longer responsible only to 'spin' the company story but also for monitoring, listening and responding to things that happen – often bringing essential information back to the company about emerging issues (and, as in the case of JetBlue, turning them into opportunities). I describe this dual function in my professional bio: 'I help companies to live their values and tell their authentic stories.'

In fact, in many cases it is essentially a no-risk proposition – because you're 'fessing up to something that people already know. JetBlue's mistake was well known by its customers, family members and was covered by the media.

Of course, it is different when the mistake is one that conflicts directly with one's stated values, but why should it be? Even if a company is 99 percent perfect, that means 1 percent of its workers might be making a mistake. Not out of malfeasance, or intention, but simply due to the fact that they are human. For larger organizations, the math plays out that for every 1,000 employees, 10 might be making a mistake. It might be major. It might be minor, but never the less, it is a mistake. Stonewalling, covering up and hiding the mistake create resentment such as that which fueled the 'United Breaks Guitars' video. The issue really wasn't that the guitar was broken, but rather the ham-fisted way in which customer service handled the situation: 'a year-long saga of pass the buck, ''don't ask me'', and ''I'm sorry sir, your claim can go nowhere.'''

So the standard is not that a company be perfect, but rather that it endeavors to act in alignment with its articulated values and, by not being afraid to admit when it falls short, increases its reputation for honesty.

In an era when transparency and authenticity are increasingly critical, it remains sound advice. As Julie Urlaub puts it, 'It's like when you Photoshop life. It might be a beautiful image, but it's not real.' She encourages companies to understand that what engages people (be they employees, customers, communities, etc.) is when companies are not afraid and let down their walls and communicate authentically and honestly.

In my experience people are pleasantly surprised – and generally open-minded – when a company no longer 'hides' behind its gates and walls (or talking points), and instead demonstrates that it is both eager and proud to share their story.

Today, we have seen the effects of a loss of public confidence not only in individual companies, but the way businesses have been operating. Stakeholders (employees, consumers, communities, investors and government regulators, and particularly for Generation Y) are becoming more and more insistent that businesses act in a manner that is socially responsible. A company that bases its culture and actions on sustainability is at a strategic advantage with stakeholders who care about these issues because this culture defines the company. The reason this is a successful strategy is because the principles of sustainability not only redefine the company as a 'good' citizen, but also because increasing stakeholder interest (demand) for corporate responsibility provides an opportunity to become a more attractive neighbor, employer, customer in addition to the preferred supplier compared with less socially conscious competitors.

PR 2.0 requires corporate communications professionals to modify their strategies, and refine the structure and content of all manner of communications vehicles from the traditional (annual reports, press releases, speeches and presentations) to the established (websites) and the evolving (social media such as Twitter, Facebook, Pinterest, YouTube, etc.) to address the issues of most concern to stakeholders.

Successful businesses increasingly relying on building and fostering open, multi-stakeholder dialogue with their key stakeholders, including their own employees, customers, communities, shareholders and investors, government regulators and legislators and yes, even their competitors.

Working with stakeholders within the organization is also important, using the employee (or internal) communications function to obtain the input and gain the buy-in of tax, legal, human resources and other departments that will benefit (and can offer important guidance) in the development of both the policies and the messages explaining them.

Additionally, since transparency requires companies to reveal their shortcomings as part of the process, the legal department is another key constituency. In order for the reporting to be transparent and credible, measurement of both the initial baselines as well as subsequent results will need to be done through internal experts, consultants, NGO partners and/or a combination. And to avoid litigation, legal professionals must be engaged to ensure that the messages do not put the organization at legal risk, particularly in light of the sometimes highly charged and litigious atmosphere that seems all too prevalent these days, particularly in the US.

But the opportunity is almost unlimited. Through digital media consumers are able to directly connect and voice their opinions to brands not in private conversations, but surrounded by the hundreds, thousands and possibly even millions who are connected through the Web. No longer can brands hide behind the wall of private communication and continue to push their stakeholder inquiries, concerns or problems aside. Brands must react, engage and build trust by interacting with their social communities – this means if you do it well, with honesty and integrity and sharing the good, the bad and even the ugly – you have the opportunity to expose your brand to a much wider constituency.

## A word about 'native advertising'

One of the consequences of the increase in digital media has been that print media have faced shrinking revenue from both of their traditional income streams: ad revenues and subscriptions. Similarly broadcast media are losing audience share and so both have turned to what is called 'native advertising' to supplement income.

Native advertising or branded marketing is a new term for an old practice – inserting advertising into the existing media alongside news stories in order to get the story out. Increasingly however, the separation between advertising and news has become blurred, with companies (and those who sell the service) doing their best to simulate news articles in such a way that audiences find it difficult to determine which items are actual news stories and which are advertising masquerading as news. Research shows that seven out of 10 visitors to sites have trouble distinguishing the difference.

Clearly, in a book about communicating authentically in the digital age, I am going to come down against any deliberate misleading of the public. The study also supports that this is a not a new business model but a short-term solution to prop up revenues: 'Native advertising on news sites degrades the trust of visitors. Its continued practice will come back to bite the very brands that employ this uneducated approach to marketing.'[9]

Sadly, even venerable and trusted news institutions have allowed their news to be infiltrated in this manner. At a recent conference,

*The New York Times'* executive vice president of advertising defended native advertising:

*Let me start by vigorously refuting the notion that native advertising has to erode consumer trust or compromise the wall that exists between editorial and advertising. Good native advertising is just not meant to be trickery. It's meant to be publishers sharing storytelling tools with marketers.*

My purpose is not to engage in a discussion on the morality, ethics or the long-term prospects for this practice to destroy the very credibility that has been the hallmark and business model of the news media, but rather to caution those considering this form of digital engagement to ask themselves if they are truly being authentic with their stakeholders.

As it happens, I believe that this is a desperate gasp of traditional media to find new revenue streams, and news outlets and perhaps even the new media companies that engage in this practice will discover that they risk destroying their credibility by engaging in a deceptive practice to disguise their marketing and advertising messages as news.

CHAPTER 5

# Social Media are Nothing New

**KEY POINTS:**

- Social media are not new; most companies use traditional social media without fear.

- You have never been in 'control' of your brand; your employees are and always have been.

- If you're worried what your employees might say about you on Twitter, your problem is not Twitter.

The companies and organizations that consider social media to be a threat to how they control their brands and messages are missing out on the larger opportunity to use these powerful tools to build their reputation through authenticity and transparency.

They also fear losing 'control' because they have failed to recognize that they never were really 'in control'. That is because a brand can never be 'controlled'. Why not? Brands are intangible assets, created by the emotions that people feel when they experience, purchase or use your products, interact with your employees, see your name on the side of a vehicle on the road and a myriad of other uncontrolled interactions that happen throughout their lifetime.

> *The companies and organizations that consider social media to be a threat to how they control their brands and messages are missing out on the larger opportunity to use these powerful tools to build their reputation through authenticity and transparency.*

A single employee had more control over Exxon's brand than the combined talents of their corporate communications department, public relations, government relations, investor relations and marketing teams combined when he came to work intoxicated and ceded control to an inexperienced crew member who steered the *Exxon Valdez* into Bligh Reef in Prince William Sound. Similarly, when Chesley 'Sully' Sullenberger III successfully glided his crippled airliner into the Hudson River, in addition to the lives of the passengers and crew, he – *and the crew on board* – also had US Airways' reputation in his hands. And while the 'brand police' might have cringed over how prominent the logo was on the side of the jet, they can take no credit for how the reputation of the company was enhanced by the heroic actions that day.

Why then are organizations drafting social media guidelines (and some even attempting to impose prohibitions) when they would never consider handing out 'communications guidelines' along with logo-ed apparel? The only difference between what someone says while wearing your brand and what they tweet is the scale and potential for social media comments to 'go viral'.

What companies fear most is the loss of control. And there have certainly been instances of that happening. But let's put it in perspective. In 2012 the average person on Twitter had only 208 followers and only followed 102 people.[10] Contrast that with the potential of a person wearing your logoed t-shirt engaging in an embarrassing action at even the poorest attended baseball game with 16,900 potential in-person witnesses[11] (not to mention those watching on TV). That was the basis of a US$10 million lawsuit filed by a fan for emotional distress[12] when he was shown napping during a New York Yankees–Boston Red Sox game. But my point here is, did anyone notice – or care – what it said on the shirt he was wearing? Or the four people also visible in the frame (wearing Yankee's caps and/or shirts)?

> *208 – The number of 'followers'*
> *the average person had on Twitter in 2012.*

And, being honest, I am going to admit right now that at some point, someone is going to say or do something on digital media that will make you question why they said or did it. But (unless what is said is illegal, threatening or in some other way unacceptable) it is important to keep it in perspective. After all, if the majority of what is said about you is positive and on-message, then how much harm has really been done? And how much more harm would be done if people were to become aware of concerted efforts to 'censor' rather than listen to one's critics? Especially when they are right.

In fact, corporate apparel *are* social (but not digital) media. And companies are so comfortable with sharing them that they give it to employees, send it as gifts to customers and even complete strangers. But if you asked recipients to sign a document agreeing what they would and would not say while wearing it, where they would and would not go and with whom they would and would not associate prior to getting the 'swag' – you'd be laughed out of the room. In fact, the comfort and recognized value of 'brand enhancement' of these items is so high companies don't even take them back when you leave company! Even if they fire you. For cause.

Face it: if you're worried what your employees might say about you on Twitter, your problem is not Twitter. And the same applies to your customers, suppliers and communities in which you operate. Even one or two outliers cannot overcome the overwhelming weight of the truth as others experience it. If your official Twitter account is the only one saying good things about you, digital media are the least of your worries.

> *If you're worried what your employees might say about you on Twitter, your problem is not Twitter.*
>
> *If your official Twitter account is the only one saying good things about you, digital media are the least of your worries.*

Fear of the negative prevents companies from taking advantage of the huge upside potential of empowering their workforce as brand ambassadors. After all, who knows you better than your employees? And if that's not something you're proud to share, your problems won't be solved by efforts to keep them quiet online. They're telling someone.

It is time for us to change the way that we think about brands and messages. It is time for dialogue with stakeholders instead of using social media as another channel to 'deliver' messages to a passive 'audience'. Proactively responding to a concern posted on Facebook (rather than removing all negative comments and turning the page into an extension of your website) creates an opportunity to demonstrate your values and brand promise.

After all, your brand is defined by the sum total of all of the experiences that people have with you that define how they feel about your organization. And remember it is possible for your good deeds to last as long – and be as tweetable – as your mistakes.

Others will say that you 'can't unring a bell' if someone says something negative about your company. All the more reason to empower those who would like to say good things about you so that (to continue the metaphor) the preponderance of the 'notes' played and heard are on key and in tempo. The one errant note becomes an outlier and is not only overshadowed, the fact that you did not overreact to it demonstrates that you are not afraid to let people speak their minds.

...................................................................................

# CHAPTER 6

# Digital Media: An Effective Tool

**KEY POINTS:**

- Relationships developed on digital media can be real.

- The focus on sustainability and the opportunity of digital media are changing the ways that people expect to be engaged.

- Whether or not your digital program is effective really depends on what you aim to achieve.

Relationships formed (or begun) online can be real. Once considered 'fringe' or even 'desperate,' online dating is now an established and respected way for people to meet. In 2013 the National Academy of Sciences found that one third of all marriages in the United States had started with online relationships. Similarly, relationships between like-minded professionals can spring from digital relationships including those through shared interest pages on sites like LinkedIn, shared subjects on Twitter, etc. Indeed my professional relationships with many of the experts and individuals that I continue to collaborate with and learn from (some of whom I have and will cite in this book – including Henk Campher, Aman Singh, Julie Urlaub, Wayne Visser to name a few) have begun online. And in the cases where we have met in person afterwards, I have been pleased to discover that the person I met online was the same as the person in real life.

As I wrote for the Huffington Post:

*Authenticity is what turns a pretty picture into a priceless work of art. Likewise it is what people look for – or should – in their personal relationships. I believe this holds true for our relationships with businesses as well; whether as consumers or employees, members of the community, or investors.*[13]

In other words, if one honestly and openly represents the company (or person) that they really are, then digital media can be a reflection of that reality and begin, sustain, and in some cases, even repair relationships.

Some data I find relevant to social media communications for building trust and ultimately affecting the brand reputation and the bottom line:

- 92% of consumers say they trust earned media, such as social media, word of mouth, recommendation from friends and family, above all other forms of advertising.[14]

- 82% of consumers trust a company more if they are involved with social media.[15]

- 77% of buyers said they are more likely to buy from a company if the CEO uses social media.[16]

Many continue to try to fit 'digital media' into familiar (and comfortable) boxes – using them as an extension of traditional marketing techniques. But sustainability and digital media are changing the ways that employees, consumers, suppliers and communities themselves engage with brand

> *It is precisely that shift – from single directional dialogue with an 'audience' to dialogue with individuals to online discussions, collaborations, arguments and even collaborations with groups and individuals who have never met in person – that defines PR 2.0 and why and how it can be so effective.*

and business and *expect those brands and businesses to engage with them!* Leading companies are finding this leads to increased brand reputation and even new revenue streams, helping to capture brand loyalty much in the same way that the iPod did for Apple.

It is precisely that shift – from single directional dialogue with an 'audience' to dialogue with individuals to online discussions, collaborations, arguments and even collaborations with groups and individuals who have never met in person – that defines PR 2.0 and why and how it can be so effective.

During the third quarter of Super Bowl XLVII when a power outage caused a partial blackout and stopped the game for about half an hour, Oreo cookie's social media team was ready. They jumped on the cultural moment by tweeting an ad that read 'Power Out? No problem' with a starkly lit image of a solitary Oreo and the caption 'You can still dunk in the dark.' The message caught on almost immediately, getting nearly 15,000 retweets, more than 20,000 likes on Facebook. How did they respond so well and so quickly? By including digital in their overall strategy which also included a regular commercial during the first half the game, they also had their social media team at the ready to respond to whatever happened online – whether it was a mind-blowing play or, as it happened, half the lights shutting off. And they were smart to wait until after the cause of the blackout was known, so that they did not seem insensitive if some tragedy had taken place.

Combining traditional and digital media is what the Queensland Department of Tourism did to increase visits to their region. Their campaign used a combination of the well-known 'Jobs' section of newspapers as well as digital media. They ran a wanted ad for the self-described 'best job in the world' which offered one lucky person AU$150,000 to spend six months cleaning the pool, feeding the fish, collecting the mail and exploring a gorgeous, little-known island off the Great Barrier Reef. All the applicants had to do was submit a one-minute video. The Board received more than 7 million visitors, 34,000 applicants from 200 countries, and 500,000 votes for this once-in-a-lifetime job.

Other examples include helping an ad go 'viral' such as the Volvo Trucks ad featuring Jean-Claude Van Damme doing a split between two semis moving at speed. Or a standalone video such as TD Bank turning their ATM into an 'automatic thanking machine'[17] – giving long-time customers gifts ranging from sports apparel and the chance to throw out the first pitch to plane tickets to visit an ailing daughter which has been shared more than half a million times via YouTube, Facebook and Twitter. (A similar idea was done by WestJet as a "Christmas Miracle.")

Keying in on cultural events (holidays) and icons is one way to turn loose the power of digital media. Another way is clever innovation, and a bit of luck, such as the ALS Ice Bucket Challenge mentioned earlier which grabbed people's imaginations – from President Bush being doused by his wife Laura to Dave Grohl of the Foo Fighters' incredibly clever shot-by-shot parody of the horror movie *Carrie* and even a collection of 'fails' where people managed to get the challenge wrong in spectacular fashion.

In the process it generated millions of dollars and increased awareness of a disease that previously was much less well known (and received far fewer donations) than cancer, heart disease, HIV/AIDS, etc. In the highly competitive world of not-for-profit advocacy this campaign literally put ALS into public consciousness and, more importantly, increased donations and the donor base of organizations fighting the disease.

A key success factor these things share is two attributes that contribute to the effectiveness of face-to-face communication – interactivity (people are moved to do something and share their experience) and immediacy; such as when businesses respond to customers' inquiries and complaints in a timely and helpful fashion on their websites or social media 'fan' pages. Another way is to host a blog where issues relating to your expertise are shared and discussed, such as the group of registered dietitians whom I helped train and empower to contribute regularly to Sodexo North America's 'health and wellness' blog. By offering regular, timely (often seasonal) advice, recipes and tips, this cadre of experts sharing healthy options became the most visited blog on the website within one year of its launch and it maintains that position today.

Ultimately, companies define what 'effectiveness' means to them. Shonali Burke, Social PR strategist who was named in *PRWeek*'s first 'top 40 under 40' list and the first list of 25 Women That Rock Social Media, points out that many of her clients want to join and participate in conversation around their area of expertise, business and knowledge, with the goal of being recognized by 'thought leaders' as appropriate and credible sources:

*This is very similar to what PR agencies were (and still are) primarily tasked with doing: Secure positive (or minimize negative) earned media, as that will (or should) beget thought leadership because a trusted source – aka the media – is highlighting them and their ideas as role models.*

> *One thing that remains consistent, just as it is true for all forms of communications, the digital 'solution' created for them has to be specifically about them, and their goals and not 'borrowed' from another organization that has made waves in digital by doing something specific.*

Along the continuum, there are companies who are already participating in the conversation, but wish to change their position. PR people refer to this as 'thought leadership elevation.' And then there are companies who have very specific outcome-based goals, and want digital to help them achieve those goals.

In short, there is no single 'right' or 'wrong' answer for how to best include digital in one's communications plans and efforts. But one thing that remains consistent, just as it is true for all forms of communications, the digital 'solution' created for them has to be specifically about them and their goals and not 'borrowed' from another organization that has made waves in digital by doing something specific.

"So whether or not your digital program is effective really depends on what you aim to achieve," concludes Burke.

And of course, being clever and using digital media in a way that takes advantage of its attributes can make all the difference:

| Attribute | Opportunity |
| --- | --- |
| Immediacy | • Respond quickly and earn a reputation for caring what people think/feel<br>• Ability to become part of things that are in the news or cultural events quickly |
| Interactivity | • Build a relationship<br>• Listen as well as share information<br>• Humanize your organization by having a personality online<br>• Take advantage of being 'live'<br>• Show that you care about things by expressing an opinion about things that your stakeholders care about – including them and their opinions |
| Visual | • Effective storytelling using pictures/images to illustrate<br>• Build relationships |

All digital media are not the same; each has its strengths and weaknesses. One common weakness that must be acknowledged is the lack of 'tone of voice' or facial expression that make things like humor, sarcasm, etc., hard to convey.

| Digital tool | Strengths | Weaknesses |
|---|---|---|
| Twitter | • Immediacy (speed)<br>• Interactive<br>• Simplicity<br>• Easy to respond<br>• Not moderated – so no control what is said about you<br>• Free | • Speed can be hard for some organizations<br>• Impossible to share truly complex concepts; even with adding hyperlinks<br>• Too easy (tempting) to respond swiftly when a more measured approach is indicated<br>• Not moderated – so no control what is said about you<br>• No 'tone of voice' so humor and/or sarcasm can backfire easily |
| Facebook | • Constituency building (fans, people who 'like' your pages, etc.) and therefore get your updates<br>• 'Closed' groups allow for teams to teambuild; including virtual and project teams<br>• Free for users<br>• User-friendly<br>• Accepts paid ads and corporate pages | • It can be very easy for multiple pages to be launched, diluting your brand message<br>• No substitute for an IntraNet for sharing best practices and ideas; Messages/ideas can 'get out'<br>• No 'tone of voice' so humor and/or sarcasm can backfire easily<br>• Paid ads are often a target for criticism; but they can be effective |

| Digital tool | Strengths | Weaknesses |
| --- | --- | --- |
| LinkedIn | • Discussion boards allow for conversations and crowdsourcing of ideas<br>• Constituency building<br>• Organizational presence facilitates recruitment | • Discussion board can be harder to navigate<br>• No 'tone of voice' so humor and/or sarcasm can backfire easily |
| YouTube | • Easy to use<br>• Can present visual content<br>• Public way to share videos<br>• Free<br>• A way to get comments and public reaction<br>• Easy to share with other users | • Not good for proprietary content (although private, non-searchable pages are an option)<br>• Slower feedback (comments, likes) than some of the other channels |
| Instagram | • Real time<br>• Visual<br>• Can be useful to showcase products or places | • Images without context subject to interpretation |
| Pinterest | • Visual<br>• Can be useful to showcase products or places | • Images without context subject to interpretation |

# CHAPTER 7

# Developing a Plan That Works

**KEY POINTS:**

- Always be prepared; include digital in your strategy and communications planning.

- Use digital media as one of the tools to achieve your business goals.

- Communications plans and metrics must address what matters to leaders for success of the business.

**FIGURE 2. Four phases of digital engagement.**

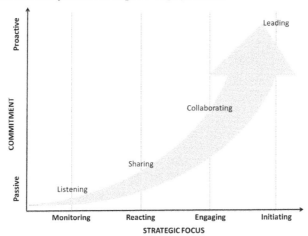

I have defined four stages that describe the maturation of a company's digital engagement efforts and the amount of commitment each requires.

| Phase | Strategy | Hallmarks/actions |
|---|---|---|
| Monitoring | Listening | • Company understands that the conversation is happening<br>• Wish to know 'what is being said about us' and by whom<br>• May hire a firm or service to monitor and analyze trends |
| Reacting | Sharing | • No discernable strategy behind outreach<br>• All messages treated as equally important<br>• Saying a lot of things but not having a clear 'voice'<br>• Labor-intensive efforts to respond individually to individual comments, tweets, posts<br>• Risk mitigation through efforts to take the conversation 'off-line' by encouraging people to send email or call |
| Engaging | Collaborating | • Focus on selected topics of expertise/interest that match corporate strategy<br>• Participate in conversations but no effort to 'steer' or control what people say, allowing the conversation to play out<br>• Comfortable enough to encourage employee participation knowing these are brand ambassadors<br>• Do not overreact to the negative comments, knowing on balance the conversation will be favorable |

| Phase | Strategy | Hallmarks/actions |
|-------|----------|-------------------|
| Initiating | Leading | • Stakeholder conversation helps (part) drive the corporate strategy to lead by listening, responding and delivering to stakeholders |
| | | • Hosting and joining conversations on issues that matter to stakeholders on own and other sites |
| | | • May or may not be the issues the company wishes to address |
| | | • Invitation to dialogue/continue conversation publicly encouraged |
| | | • Comfortable enough to encourage employee participation knowing these are brand ambassadors |

Giving lip service to strategy is a danger I see in corporate communications when it comes to digital efforts. Initially the promise was made to 'catch some customers' in the Web (an internal promotional piece for a company's first website in the mid-1990s showed people literally caught in a spider web!) and that promise is still being made. But too many do it amorphously. I recently heard the head of corporate communications declare that the purpose of the corporate website was to 'drive sales.' But there was no effort to match the structure and function of the site to the articulated goal. Nowhere on the site was the 'buy here' or a 'click here to be contacted by your local representative' button. The only exception was the careers page, which clearly offered a mechanism to upload a resume or CV and set a job alert. The site requires potential customers to back out from wherever they are when they are inspired to act (even on pages dedicated to specific products and services) and go to the main page to find and use the general contact number to phone the company. A best practice from outside the industry (such as Amazon or eBay) would have offered a more effective model if the true goal of the website is to drive and facilitate sales.

Likewise in media relations, we hear often that 'the press release is dead.' It is not dead, but it is no longer the standalone or exclusive tool. Companies know if they put them out 'Google alerts' all over the company will deliver regular examples of just how much their communications department is communicating. While aggregator websites do not drive public opinion, the media still relies heavily on newswire-distributed press releases to find news and reference information, according to recent findings from *Business Wire*. Nearly 70% of journalists responding to the 2014 Business Wire Media Survey stated that their jobs would be *more difficult* if newswire-distributed press releases were no longer available.

But increasingly only as part of an overall strategy: today company's online newsrooms are the foremost destination (after the main website) for journalists when they need to research an organization. More than 50% of the media surveyed said online newsrooms should be updated frequently, anywhere from hourly to several times per day.

But it is important to note that organizational social networks tied for second most effective with official spokespersons.[18] It makes sense; after all, who knows an organization better than those who work there? That assumed credibility is another strong argument for turning employees loose as brand ambassadors with the empowerment to participate. Of course, in theory, if you are living your strategy they would already have that information. In the areas of ethics, the environment, corporate

HR policies, etc., they know the values you are living because they experience them every day. If those values are the same as the ones on the corporate office walls and website, then this is another powerful way to reach the public directly as well as through the media.

Digital engagement is about building authentic and credible relationships online. Henk Campher offers this caution: "Even when they 'get this' too many think that engaging *around their issues* are real engagement." He points out that for many companies "there is no real interest in engaging with their target audiences around *topics of interest to the target audience.*" If your digital efforts are exclusively aligned with promoting your business objectives, you are missing the power of digital to truly engage with people. "Don't push messages and don't engage only around issues only of interest to you. Find their interests and engage around those as well," he advises.[19]

Aman Singh, a digital and social media strategist with experience writing for *Forbes* and running editorial operations across the CSRwire platform (among other media outlets) offers this advice about reaching the audience where it is; "This might mean writing three or four smaller blogs rather than one long press release that tries to emote and connect via quotes from key leaders and a few numbers."

She is also a fan of Twitter, when used properly:

*The first channel that comes to mind is Twitter. There's the connectivity aspect where you can now reach your stakeholders without the boundaries of emails, surveys or cold calls. Then there are Twitter chats, which offer a unique, succinct and powerful way to engage multiple stakeholders. From an organizational viewpoint, Twitter offers a platform to not just publish but also engage meaningfully. Once you go beyond the 'pop culture' perception of Twitter, it is a useful medium to reach a cross section of people if the goal is engagement versus distribution.*

Take for example SC Johnson, the company that makes Windex, Ziploc and Draino. They make a lot of products that don't necessarily make you think of being green or sustainable, but while they make these traditional products, they have sustainability goals to engage consumers in making greener choices. They use their Twitter stream to build connections and partnerships online. Their global corporate affairs, communications and sustainability teams tweet their environmental topics, tips and green choices tweets from their @SCJGreenChoices Twitter account. And they make it easy, fun and engaging, such as this tweet:

*@SCJGreenChoices #GreenTrivia question: How many times can #aluminum beverage cans be recycled?*

Which they followed sometime later with the answer:

*@SCJGreenChoices #GreenTrivia answer: Aluminum beverage cans are 100% recyclable and can be recycled forever! @CansRecyclable*

Another thing that they do very well is how they interact with their followers, offering tips that others share, crediting those stakeholders:

*@SCJGreenChoices Valentine's may have passed but this breakfast is still a great way to save mileage and stay home: bit.ly/1eNUsSP from @alisonlewis*

This is a strategic move because they are leveraging Alison's Twitter network of more than 7,000 followers. What makes those followers important to SC Johnson, is that Alison is a 'TV Spokesperson, Founder & Editor in Chief for Healthy Travel Magazine, and a Wellness Travel Blogger for Huffington Post, Author, Recipe Developer/Mom of 3.' All commonalities within SC Johnson's target audience for their products.

The lessons here are that SC Johnson builds connections and partnerships online by sharing blog posts, pictures, tips and green ideas not only from their own company but also from other like-minded individuals, businesses, and organizations that are important to them and their business. They are using the power of digital media to build better social relationships with partners, prospects and consumers while also increasing brand loyalty by advancing the sustainability conversation.

## A note about Twitter chats

Twitter chats can generate a great deal of engagement, and should be planned like any other presentation or event; including talking points, key messages, supporting information (including links), etc. And because the medium is limited in length to 140 characters (and can come very swiftly); I recommend being ready to explain 'too hard to explain in 140 chars, will follow up...' and offer a blog (if many people are asking the same or similar question) or promise to respond to them directly (via email or private message) to answer. People using the various platforms are used to this and understand why it can be necessary, but only make these promises if you are prepared to respond in a timely fashion. Failing to do so will be perceived as uncaring (at best) or avoiding an issue (at worst).

Corporate communications professionals must use their skills to articulate the organization's environmental, social and as well as the more traditional economic commitments to all of these groups and be prepared to discuss actual performance against goals and objectives. Aspirational goals are often explained through standards or statements of expectations (including financial goals and forecasts, ethics, environmental and safety policies).

Just as I advise communications professionals to engage with stakeholders about what matters to them, they must take this advice when developing their communications plans and metrics for success. Measures such as Facebook 'likes', Twitter 'followers' and even 'impressions' have little resonance in the company boardroom.

Working with and engaging with stakeholders offers insight into how to ensure that these policies not only reflect community needs and values but also industry standards as well as any statutory and regulatory requirements. In other words, expectations of what is reasonable can be managed, provided the dialogue is open, transparent and authentic.

Digital media allows for crowdsourcing and collective intelligence to solve problems. That means admitting the best ideas may not always be within your organization. Want to be the preferred employer? You would do well to look outside your industry to see what the best of the best are doing? Even better, look (and listen) to what people are asking for. Want to know how to improve your supply chain logistics? Look outside your industry – as a building materials company did by looking for best practices not only within the same industry but also looking at the acknowledged leaders in distribution – in package and pizza delivery.

Sometimes the best ideas come from unexpected places. And we have to be open to them.

Why does it matter? Because increasingly people are looking to business to solve the problems that business faces (and in some cases has created).

While we have a development model that works at improving quality of life (as measured by longevity, health, financial prosperity) we must face the sobering reality that we haven't figured out how to do that without sacrificing the environment in the process, and the benefits of this progress have not been universally shared, and have sometimes been achieved at the expense of the less fortunate. And if we do not find a way to lift people out of poverty, provide economic opportunity and improve health and longevity within the capacity of the Earth to regenerate itself, we will eventually run out of resources to continue to help people and, quite possibly risk passing a 'tipping point' at which we end up not only reversing the progress we have made, but reducing the standard of living for all of us. And if we do not find a model that more equitably shared those benefits across all nations and socio-economic levels, we may find that people run out of patience before we run out of resources. Remember the uprising in Egypt was fueled, in large part, by a lack of economic opportunity among a large majority of the population.

Julie Urlaub's successful sustainability practice (Taiga Company) is based on the belief that social media engagement tools offer an 'evolved approach to stakeholder **participation**' (emphasis added). By expanding the scope of contributors and encouraging increased feedback, a decision-maker opens the 'suggestion box' to a variety of untapped viewpoints.

1. **Have a clear vision of why you want to engage online**: What are your social media goals? Is it to increase website/blog traffic? Promote brand image and credibility? Communicate and engage on sustainability related topics? Clearly identify your traditional sales objectives combined with your sustainability metrics and design a social media marketing strategy that delivers results to both.

2. **Know who matters!** Identify stakeholders and online communities to reach them. Stakeholders are a bit easier to identify, as long as one is careful to define stakeholders as 'those who have a vested interest in the continued (long term) success of your business as part of their agenda'. Consider employees, customers, suppliers, partners, local communities, shareholders, regulator and legislators, the media and other opinion leaders and NGOs. Another often overlooked group is competitors. While you won't want to share competitive intelligence and corporate secrets, competitors are more interested in ensuring the mutual vested industry in where your entire industry is going and how it fares.

In fact, they are more important stakeholders than short-term investors, anti-business advocates and those who are fundamentally against the continuation and/or growth of your particular business or industry.

One effective strategy to engage with a larger number of people (and organizations) interested in a specific issue or centered on sustainability concepts such as recycling, corporate responsibility, water, energy, social investing, etc., is through online communities. Or, they may be geographically based.

3. **Be committed.** You can't just put your toe in the water. Digital media are always 'on' and being present means being part of the conversation. That means: listening, contributing to the conversation, providing timely feedback, and incorporating that information into products, services and ongoing dialog.

As Urlaub says; "Success is no longer defined by how well your company communications its message to the external world. It is rapidly becoming a critical business sustainability skill and a business sustainability catalyst that is affecting the bottom line."[20]

Lastly, there is a tremendous volume of information and interaction on digital media. It is overwhelming and a lot of what some companies are doing is adding to the volume of noise, answering every 'tweet' and responding to every Facebook post as if they are all 'life and death' situations. Again this often stems from the fear of an unanswered complaint going viral a la 'United Breaks Guitars.' But that is exhausting for those responsible for monitoring and responding and ultimately is the sign of a very poorly formed strategy. After all, not every critic is credible, not every complaint requires a public response, as tempting as it may be. I was once asked to respond to someone who had been critical about a company on a blog post but, upon reflection and research, I was able to determine that the page had had less than a dozen page views. Knowing that that number was bound to increase exponentially if the organization responded with its full weight, I recommended that they strategically to allow it to pass unanswered.

But at the same time we were ready to respond if necessary if the story did go wider.

I have the same situation happen on my Twitter feed, where those representing advocacy organizations will attempt to 'bait' me into responding. Because my Twitter account represents my personal brand, I respond patiently and politely. But I refuse to engage with people who indulge in personal attacks or who are clearly trying to gain attention and increase their profile simply by having me respond to them.

Likewise, I never retweet something that I have not read or with which I do not agree; unless it is to point out that fact. I find the statement 'retweets are not endorsements' to be rather confusing – if you don't believe something, why say it? And that goes for companies trying to establish their presence online. One cannot develop the reputation as a thought leader simply by retweeting. Instead, have a voice, state your opinions and stand by them. I liken it to walking around a party following behind a popular person and repeating verbatim everything that they say. That's not going to impress people.

> *Have a voice, state your opinions and stand by them.*

# CHAPTER 8

# Building an Internal Constituency Including Selling It Upstairs

**KEY POINTS:**

- Digital media are powerful, when used as part of an overall communications plan.

- Selling digital requires that it be an effective way to serve a larger purpose; not just doing something for its own sake.

- Starting small, and achieving a success for others, is the best way to build buy in for digital media.

One of the challenges communicators face when advocating the use of digital media is the paradox that people alternatively fear the power of digital media and, on the other hand, find it frivolous. They are questioning how things like tweets can really drive brand value while at the same time fearing that something negative will 'go viral' and destroy brand value.

To the first point, I like to point out that while Twitter can seem to be quite simplistic – with short messages – it can have a great place in a communications effort *when used in combination with other tools*. Many powerful messages such as 'Houston, we've had a problem' (Apollo 13) to the note that alerted the world to the plight of 33 miners in Chile and resulted in their rescue; 'Estamos bien en el refugio, los 33,' required far fewer than 140 characters. But, as I mentioned, those short notes were effective only because they were *part of a larger context.*

Shaping that larger context is critical. Shonali Burke takes it back to the core question: "How do you know if you are moving the needle? That all depends on which needle you wish to move."

*Engagement is an important piece of the continuum, from awareness to engagement and ideally to action. But what does engagement really mean? People are talking with you, but is that what engagement is ... or is it simply acknowledgement (retweets, likes) and how does that get them to action?*

Aman Singh offers this advice, based on her three years of experience at CSRwire, facilitating a number of Twitter 'chats' for a cross-section of corporations and nonprofits. "As a facilitator and a communicator, I measure engagement: number of questions asked, participation numbers, feedback, impact as well as the ripple effect, i.e., what happened in the weeks to follow [media pickup, feedback, traffic, mentions, questions, etc.]."

She encourages the same approach when approaching executives, pointing out that numbers rarely tell the whole story. "There's the story behind the numbers – the feedback, the knowledge sharing, the best practices, the public relations and the true impact. For many, these have continued for months after the chat occurred."

She points out that chats she has moderated led to awards recognizing the companies for transparency. "For some like Sodexo and Unilever, these have led to increased engagement, readership and brand loyalty."

And of course digital media are watched by, and can influence, traditional media. Singh conducted a first-of-its-kind chat with Kimberly-Clark and Greenpeace in August 2014 bringing both organizations together to describe their evolution from adversaries to collaborators following Greenpeace's Kleercut campaign in 2009. The chat not only brought more than 200 people together for an hour and generated millions in impressions; it also spilled over into more mainstream media like Ad Age.

## Getting employees on board

Shonali Burke points out that so many PR efforts are outward-facing it is easy to overlook the importance of empowering employees.

She cautions against creating a digital strategy and imposing it. "Don't just create one and plunk it on them saying, 'Here you go, this is what we're doing in digital.'" At the same time you give them a voice, you need to manage the process, so that it doesn't turn into chaos. "Find out what the business goals for their department are, and what they think of digital. If you ask people how they think about something, as opposed to telling them what's going to happen, they're likely to be more receptive when they are presented with a plan."

She also points out that employees will have varying level of interest and competence at digital from their own social media lives. "Even if their job function is not a Communication-related function, they might be extremely creative and teach you a thing or two!"

These digital mavens, in addition to giving you some great ideas, can add to your digital team, to help with content – such as bloggers, for example. "All this only helps you scale your company's communication efforts, and you'll have the added advantage of having secured buy-in from around the table . . . because you made them feel involved."

## The C-suite

Shifting executive mindsets takes time and can be intimidating. One key to successfully presenting any strategy to executives and management teams is to understand and adopt the mindset of those executives. What matters to them – and how you can help to achieve their business goals. For example, year after year, large numbers of executives cite reputation as a top reason their companies address sustainability; of the 13 core activities surveyed by McKinsey in 2014, they believed that reputation had the most value potential for their industries.[21] Four out of ten ranked 'communicating company's sustainability activities to consumers' as being the most important to maximize financial value and one third cited 'building external stakeholder relationships' (see the discussion on intangible assets starting on page 20 in Chapter 3: Sustainability as a Business Strategy).

## Do's and Don'ts

### Things to do

1. **Know the context.** Know what is going on within your company (or the company you're advising)? Realistically identify the short- and long-term business objectives that social media strategies can support. Are there gaps in communications with stakeholders that social media can address on key issues to educate or inform stakeholders on ongoing sustainability issues? Are there missed opportunities that digital outreach can fill or help fill? During this

discovery phase, use business terms that they understand, and not social media jargon.

2. **Know the players.** The critical factor is getting all players from different departments in the organization to the table. Discover what the immediate needs and concerns are for each. What are their fears and concerns? What are their specific business needs or concerns about digital media?

3. **Develop a plan that meets their needs.** Build into your plan mid- and long-term objectives showing how digital media can support efforts to achieve their department goals now and going forward, using both hard (i.e. sales) and soft (i.e. Facebook 'likes' and Twitter 'followers') metrics. Having this data can be invaluable in moving the pilot program towards a full commitment to social media for sustainability communications. Planning is essential. Know what you are hoping to accomplish and make sure you do your homework. If you're using a digital platform for an event, for example, make sure it meets your needs and can handle the traffic, etc. Have contingency plans. What will you do and how will you handle it if people start asking things 'off topic'? Will you use a moderator to 'guide' the conversation? What will you do about negative feedback? One of the worst things a company can do is remove all criticism from its Facebook page or blog. Instead, what is your plan for responding? Will you ask to 'take the conversation off line' or transparent engage in public (a stronger response)?

4. **Define and agree on how you will measure success.** Most executives don't buy into something completely new all the way. But nothing succeeds like success. Suggest a pilot program that

will demonstrate the power and build credibility for digital media. Establish a program with less cost and more tangible results. Be clear on expectations and, most of all, clearly define how you are going to evaluate the success of the program.

5. **Report back.** Demonstrating success means you have to report back on the results of the engagement. A recent example was a Twitter chat that I was able to convince management (with the help of Aman) to 'try'. While they may have initially been interested in the potential – and later the reality – of the millions of 'impressions' from the chat (a 'softer' metric), they were also far more interested in – and impressed by – the 370% increase in year-over-year traffic to the corporate website and annual report.

## Things to avoid

1. **Don't go for broke.** The biggest mistake I see is people trying to make a big splash and impress. It is tempting when you (finally) have the ear of executives. But remember, a small success will encourage executives to invest more in your programs to generate even more success. Sometimes the best approach, particularly with those who may be skeptical or reluctant (or fearful) is to moderate your expectations. Don't try to sell an entire digital campaign. It is far better to demonstrate success at something that matters to them, and have them come to you with 'what else can you do for me/us/the company?'

2. **Don't treat everything as important.** Have your facts. Most executives, even those who may have taken calculated risks, didn't get where they are today by making impulsive choices. If

you're asked something you do not know, don't guess. Offer to get the information and get back to them. Don't consider that a 'deal breaker' – sometimes their comfort zone relies more on knowing that you are going to do a thorough and thoughtful job, and less on you having all the answers. And when dealing with information coming *in* via digital media, one of the first things that a digital communications strategist can do for any company, according to Shonali, is 'at very least, we need to help cull the volume of mentions to determine what really matters'.

3. **Do not over-sell or use metrics that may or may not matter to your leaders.** I often point at that things like 'impressions' represent the maximum potential 'audience', explaining that they indicate the total number of people who *might* have seen the story/blog/ tweet. I draw the familiar comparison that, like circulation figures for newspapers or viewership numbers for TV shows, these numbers represent the maximum potential 'audience'. I give them those numbers, of course, but concentrate on the usually smaller and more defined successes, like the number of downloads of an annual report, positive news stories (and in which media and markets) and the like.

4. **Do not consider being 'challenged' as a personal affront.** Business leaders are analytical and to many 'the bottom line is the bottom line.' A challenge means that they're thinking about it. Answer completely, honestly and as transparently as possible – even if you have to admit you don't know or that things didn't go perfectly (i.e. if a Twitter chat includes negative comments, etc.). You can put that in context, explaining both the opportunity to

solicit feedback from stakeholders, etc., and how you handled it. And even how others on the chat responded to your willingness to address your critics (and those who joined you in defending your company).

# Conclusion

**KEY POINTS:**

- Responding to digital opportunities means having and following a digital strategy that is part of your overall strategy.

- Digital media are an effective means of moving from information distribution to meaningful engagement.

- Keeping digital in mind is a good – and easy – habit to get into.

Having a strategy for digital is so important that I am coming back to it here. There is an element of chance – what will go 'viral' is the same as hoping that a traditional ad campaign will 'catch on' or that a product will become the 'it' item to have this shopping season. There are things you can do to try to facilitate these things but in the end, some succeed based on external events or the *zeitgeist*. From the downright silly (pet rocks) to the poignant (the AIDS quilt), what catches cultural fancy varies and is often unpredictable.

*Digital is not a strategy it and of itself. It must be incorporated into, and support, the overall communications plan, including having a purpose for which digital is suited. We should never let the availability of digital media tools become the driver for their use. We must continue to bring communications strategy and discipline to our efforts, knowing that some things do not lend themselves well to digital outreach.*

Digital is not a strategy it and of itself. It must be incorporated into, and support, the overall communications plan, including having a purpose for which digital media are suited. That requires that the purpose be established first, not simply to have a digital component for the sake of having one. Just as PowerPoint made it easy for anyone to create a presentation, we should never let the availability of digital media tools become the driver for their use. We must continue to bring communications strategy and discipline to our efforts, knowing that some things do not lend themselves well to digital outreach. When that is the case, it is far better to concentrate our efforts (and resources) on other ways to get our messages out.

## Establishing a digital media 'voice' by embracing and using the first person

Businesses are seen as impersonal 'things.' This is the basis behind the familiar corporate mascots and logos, to 'humanize' the company, or express something that demonstrates its values. Familiar examples include the natural (like Walt Disney using their iconic Mickey Mouse as spokesperson for the company) to those created expressly for this purpose. Similarly they can have a personality and 'voice' all their own. Some do this with the celebrities ranging from iconic faces and voices to the phenomenon of the 'celebrity CEO,' including Lee Iacocca for Chrysler and Jack Welch for GE to the more contemporary Indra Nooyi for PepsiCo and Richard Branson for the Virgin Group.

Many companies do not have – or wish to have – a single person identified as their icon. But by using the first person in communications, you not only personalize your relationship – moving from saying 'they' to 'we' from 'their' to 'our' – you also are taking responsibility; these are 'our' products, made by 'us' for 'you.' George Zimmer's; 'You're going to like the way you like, I guarantee it' for Men's Warehouse is an example, but so is GE's '**We** bring good things to light,' a great example of a value statement in the first person that uses the plural but maintains the first person. It also is a clever pun on their light bulbs for which they are perhaps best known to the lay public.

> *I applied this principle for my own personal 'branding' and came up with my Twitter and Huffington Post mini-bios:*
>
> *'I help companies live their values and tell their authentic stories.'*

## Focus on what you do, not what you make

Businesses often get caught up in production – of course, because that is how they measure output which is a key indicator of growth and success. But it causes them to miss the point that what they make only matters to them; it is what it is used for and how those products (or services) impact people that matters to the people who use their products and/ or services.

I have helped a number of organizations that are focused on what they do and I encourage them to think about the purpose and use of their efforts. For a health care measurement and advocacy organization I noted that they had more than a decade's worth of research showing that their metrics were actually improving access to care (that which is measured gets done). Working with a team and an agency, I offered up what became their new message: 'measuring quality, improving healthcare,' moving beyond the what-they-make (measurement) to the what-they-do and why-people-should-care (the improvements directly benefit people).

Similarly, I helped a large multinational construction materials company focus on what its materials were used for, shifting from typical investor-focused corporate language about its size and listing the products that they produced (some of which were incomprehensible to anyone except an industry expert) to focusing on how those materials are used and the benefits they bring – safe, attractive, comfortable spaces where people live their lives.

I was proud of the fact that the tagline that summarized this concept was used for many years. It also changed the images in the annual report and eventually on the website when the company went digital, showing people using and enjoying those spaces, rather than images of large industrial plants.

In other words, it did more than change others' image of the organizations; in each of these cases it changed *how they saw themselves*. And then they were ready to tell their story.

## Empower people

Employees are your best and most important (and credible) advocates. That is why that it is vital that they understand the role that they can and should play in promoting their organization.

The most effective way to engage people and drive behavior is by empowering them. Rather than 'name and shame,' use the 'know and show' model, demonstrating what you want them to do and the benefit of doing it. Make it simple and rewarding. Just as the numbers going down on a scale do more to encourage someone to continue dieting than all those (hopefully) well-intended people remarking about their weight.

This is particularly true for environmental and/or social concerns that appear to be huge and daunting and disempower people who may think 'what I do won't matter.' But, like the public service campaigns to 'Take a Bite Out of Crime' or 'Only You Can Prevent Forest Fires' these big issues can be broken down into simple, clear, direct messages that do not 'talk down' or 'guilt' people for prior behavior but instead offer positive reinforcement by showing them WHAT they can do, HOW they can do it, WHY it matters – and most importantly that they CAN make a difference.

Imagine your entire workforce talking about how their work and company benefit people, planet and prosperity. That's powerful.

## Get into the digital habit

Whenever I am asked to give a presentation, I not only write my remarks with the participants (not audience) in mind, I also take the time to come up with two or three key points that I wish to make and distill them down to fewer than 140 characters. Why? So that those who are attending can and will tweet them outside the room.

And I always tell the other people with whom I am planning the engagement that I am going to do that during preparation calls and meetings. And yet there's always someone who finds it surprising that I do this – even at a meeting about effective digital communications! At the Sustainable Brands conference in San Diego in 2014, I explained this strategy to my fellow panelists and even went as far as to use indicator phrases to let people know that I was going to make a key point (a standard interview and communication technique) but letting them know it would be tweetable, such as 'you challenged me to get this point down to 140 characters, so here it is . . .' and replacing the familiar 'if you remember nothing else we say here today, remember this . . .' with 'the one thing I hope you remember, and tweet, is . . .'

At this point, it is an ingrained habit. Did you notice that the key points from each chapter are fewer than 140 characters long? They are meant as 'tweetable' factoids, summarizing the content of each chapter. Were they effective in getting you to read the chapter? That's the whole point of Twitter; while it is hard (sometimes impossible) to say everything in that limited a space, it is enough to share a single, well-considered idea. And it is certainly enough to encourage someone to click on a link to a story, video or picture and to open up a dialogue. I hope it worked in this context, because that would demonstrate how I am using the principles of PR 2.0 to promote this book about PR 2.0. I would be pleased (and proud) if you were to tweet or quote any (or other ideas) that resonated with you. Please attribute them to **@johnfriedman** and #PR2.0. And yes, it can be just that easy to include a digital aspect into your efforts to *engage with people and share ideas.*

# Notes

1. http://www.theguardian.com/sustainable-business/2014/jun/03/sustainable-brands-live-from-san-diego

2. http://www.alsa.org/news/media/press-releases/ice-bucket-challenge-082214.html

3. http://www.forbes.com/sites/susanadams/2014/01/20/trust-in-business-isnt-any-better-but-trust-in-government-gets-even-worse/

4. http://blog.taigacompany.com/blog/sustainability-business-life-environment/are-social-media-relationships-real

5. Corporate Valuation for Portfolio Investment: Analyzing Assets, Earnings, Cash Flow, Stock Price, Governance, and Special Situations, ©2010.

6. http://sheltongrp.com/downloads/eco-pulse-2014/

7. Interview with the author portions of which were included published piece: http://www.huffingtonpost.com/john-friedman/csr-20-prescription-for-a_b_4955915.html

8. http://managementhelp.org/blogs/crisis-management/2011/01/31/storing-good-will/#sthash.Bu1pSmUo.dpuf

9. http://www.zdnet.com/study-on-native-advertising-finds-benefits-for-brands-risks-for-publishers-7000031978/

10. http://news.yahoo.com/twitter-statistics-by-the-numbers-153151584.html

11. http://espn.go.com/mlb/attendance

12. http://boston.cbslocal.com/2014/07/07/report-fan-who-slept-during-red-sox-yankees-game-now-suing-espn-mlb-for-mockery/

13. http://www.huffingtonpost.com/john-friedman/authenticity-offers-its-o_b_5620933.html

14. http://webbedfeet.com.au/influence-social-media-travel/

15. 6 Ways Brands Build Trust, Forbes, 31 October 2012 http://www.forbes.com/sites/brentgleeson/2012/10/31/6-ways-brands-build-trust-through-social-media/

16. 6 Ways Brands Build Trust, Forbes, 31 October 2012 http://www.forbes.com/sites/brentgleeson/2012/10/31/6-ways-brands-build-trust-through-social-media/

17. Watch the video here: http://www.ijreview.com/2014/07/162163-bank-uses-atms-say-thanks-regular-customers-personalized-heartfelt-way/

18. http://go.businesswire.com/business-wire-media-survey-results

19. Interview with the author for this publication.

20. http://blog.taigacompany.com/blog/sustainability-business-life-environment/communicating-sustainability-on-social-media-the-right-and-wrong-way

21. http://www.mckinsey.com/insights/sustainability/sustainabilitys_strategic_worth_mckinsey_global_survey_results

Lightning Source UK Ltd.
Milton Keynes UK
UKHW010854070321
379882UK00011B/1754